NEUTRALIZING DIS-EASE

MINDFULNESS-BASED AUTHORIZED CURRICULUM
2022 FIRST EDITION

Clifford L. Carter, USNV
INNER WARRIOR SPIRIT founder &
creator of NEUTRALIZING DIS-EASE

MINDFULNESS MEDITATION PROGRAM

Acknowledgments

I offer deep appreciation to the twenty-five-plus years of study and practice over the world, as well as the many teachers, both young and old, who've influenced my journey and informed this profound curriculum.

Neutralizing Dis-Ease
Mindfulness-Based Authorized Curriculum
Clifford L. Carter, USNV
September 2022 ~ First Edition

2018 © All Rights Reserved, Neutralizing Dis-Ease Mindful Based Curriculum is the intellectual property of Clifford L. Carter and may not be copied, distributed, or transferred to any individual or any organization in any form or medium without written permission. Please direct all correspondence regarding the Authorized Curriculum to Clifford L. Carter.

2022 © Images and quotes are the intellectual property of Clifford L. Carter and are not to be reproduced, copied, or distributed in any form or medium.

Without limiting the rights under copyright reserved above, no part of this publication may be reproduced, stored in or introduced into retrieval system, or transmitted, in any form or by any means (electronic, mechanical, photocopying, recording, or otherwise), including mediums not yet invented at time of publication, without prior written permission from both the copyright owner and the publisher of this book.

All images, texts, and copyrighted materials included in this book are the personal property of the author or the author has been given permission to use.

For information regarding permission, email Lionheart Group Publishing: permissions@lionheartgrouppublishing.com

Cover by Sandra Miller

ISBN: 978-1-938505-63-8

Companion Curriculum to
Neutralizing Dis-Ease Course Material
Available Fall 2023

10 9 8 7 6 5 4 3 2

Published by Lionheart Group Publishing, Eaton, Colorado, USA

Published in the USA ~ All rights reserved.

visit us on the web at www.lionheartgrouppublishing.com

Mindfulness Meditation Program

THE PYRAMID OF NEUTRALIZING DIS-EASE

NEUTRALIZING DIS-EASE

TABLE OF CONTENTS

PROLOGUE IX

COURSE OVERVIEW XI

ORGANIZATIONAL DETAILS XV

ORIENTATION SESSION XIX

CLASS ONE: EYE SENSE 1

CLASS TWO: EAR SENSE 9

CLASS THREE: NOSE SENSE 17

CLASS FOUR: TASTE SENSE 25

CLASS FIVE: TOUCH SENSE 33

CLASS SIX: THINKING MIND 41

CLASS SEVEN: THE MIND 49

CLASS EIGHT: ACTION 57

CLASS NINE: ACCEPTANCE 65

CLASS TEN: LETTING GO 73

CLASS ELEVEN: WRAP UP 81

CLASS EVALUATION FORM 89

ABOUT THE AUTHOR 93

> *"Who we are starts on the inside and slowly works its way to the surface."*

Mindfulness facilitated by the practice of breath-focused meditation is the essence of one's own inner transformation. Becoming aware of our senses leads to our understanding of self. Self-awareness leads to freedom.

One's own knowledge is ever evolving, so to say 'this is the way, the only way, the right way' is to view and understand life as static.

The truth is, life is fluid. Understanding is fluid and moves around, over, under, and sometimes even through obstacles to gain further knowledge.

A static mind travels only as far as a static obstacle arises, and then stops as it comes in contact with its enclosure.

A truly free mind experiences freedom in all directions, simultaneously gaining the necessary knowledge to find one's ultimate truth.

NEUTRALIZING DIS-EASE

MINDFULNESS-BASED AUTHORIZED CURRICULUM ~ FIRST EDITION

COURSE OVERVIEW

AFTER THREE DECADES OF MINDFULNESS practice, and more than ten years of developing and teaching *Neutralizing Dis-Ease* to hundreds of participants, I created this curriculum with the hope that others can follow the life-changing approach to mindfulness using insight meditation. As we go through eleven weeks of classroom structure, we will learn about pairing mindfulness meditation, senses, and how the mind works for and against us at every turn.

Insight meditation is simply seeing within. We will be seeing within, and also noticing sensations both inside and outside our body, using our breath as the stable and mind-calming affect it has on one's nervous system. In addition to the thinking mind, we'll learn how to observe our five senses without getting attached to or detached from one of the senses.

We'll also learn to bring the practice into the world, as any great practice should translate into our daily life. Without a translation, we become tied to our space at home—quiet, calm, structured, etc. That's not how the world truly is for most of us. I bridge that gap by starting on the cushion, creating what I call 'sitting with our uncomfortableness', then expanding the practice into the world.

Neutralizing Dis-Ease

The effects of the practice of mindfully going through each sense is truly transformational. By the end of eleven weeks, you'll have become aware of your true nature by way of your senses, in a way you have yet to comprehend. As an observer, we have the opportunity to sit without judgment: good, bad, happy, sad. We are simply experiencing a moment in time truly accepting just as we are.

CLIFFORD L. CARTER

"Today belongs to yesterday's cause."

Clifford L. Carter

Neutralizing Dis-Ease

Mindfulness-Based Authorized Curriculum ~ First Edition

Organizational Details

Below are organizational details about various topics including class size, location, materials, length, time in between class, etc. Please note these are suggestions. We understand, and the core of our program is, everything changes. So, we are consistently faced with changing circumstance. These details are merely a jumping-off point based on past class experiences and certainly not written for the purpose of a hard-fast rule.

❈ Course meets once a week.

❈ Course last for a duration of eleven weeks.

❈ Each class meets for 1 to 1 1/2 hrs.

❈ Class includes five sense-awareness practices, including the thinking mind. These are explored in depth, one sense per week.

❈ Sitting meditation.

❈ Walking meditation.

❈ Exploring how the mind grasps and averts.

❈ Acceptance practice.

❋ Letting go, and the concepts of the body and *letting go*.

❋ A process is added to every class for depth of understanding.

❋ Class size should be limited to fifteen participants.

What to wear and bring: Comfortable clothing should be worn. Something to write with and to write on would be beneficial for taking notes. We've included a small section at the end of each chapter for that purpose. Food or drink is not recommended during the sensations instruction, as we are working with each sensation—meaning the other senses will have less of a focus.

Daily practice homework is encouraged, to include meditation focused on the breath and contemplating the sensation from the previous class.

Clifford L. Carter

"Being is not about movement either way. It is not about action. It is about okayness. Being into a situation without the need to change or alter the outcome for myself or the participants."

Clifford L. Carter

Neutralizing Dis-Ease

Mindfulness-Based Authorized Curriculum ~ First Edition

Orientation Session

Overview

❋ Introducing participants, including their meditation experience(s).

❋ Encourage participants to fully embrace the *Mindfulness Meditation Program* (MMP) practice while abandoning past practice(s) during the time of this course.

❋ Give brief overview of class using class Overview and Prologue.

Recommended Time

❋ 1 to 1 1/2 hours to cover material and practice.

Mindfulness Meditation

❋ Insight meditation, focusing on the breath and becoming aware of sensations inside and outside the body.

Brief Sharing

❋ Sharing of experiences.

❋ Dispel stuck points.

❋ Encourage practice.

Class Sequence

❋ Overview of ORIENTATION with PROLOGUE.

❋ Introductions and Experience.

❋ Myths and Stuck Points.

❋ Practice Instructions.

❋ Brief Sitting Meditation Practice.

❋ Sharing of Experience.

❋ Dispel Stuck Points.

❋ Encourage Practice.

❋ Questions and Answers.

Class Content

❋ Learning through experiential process including all aspects of class sequence.

❋ Encourage home practice between class.

❋ The use of outside experiential learning tools to facilitate sensation process. To be described in each class description.

Participating Guidelines for Attendees

✵ This is a secular program, meaning there is no religious affiliation bound by or favoring this program.

✵ The only requirement is a willingness to see within one's self. Meaning, transformation comes from a place of questioning. Not knowing and being open to the possibilities we have yet to find and not yet experienced, whether outside or deep inside one's self.

✵ Class participation is encouraged for the benefit of the others, while sharing a connected experience has great transformational benefit for all.

Inherent Benefit

✵ Mindfulness meditation, when practiced daily, can calm the nervous system and can help us make more clear decisions in the moment.

✵ Meditation practice slows the mind so we can focus our attention on an object.

✵ Insight meditation is looking inward, gaining one's own insight or understanding of self.

✵ Viewing sensations as neutral gives us the ability to become less triggered by incoming stimuli.

✵ The ability to take MMP practice into the world enables us to continue our efforts, not only while we sit on the cushion but as we are moving through our daily life. As challenges arise, we have tools to manage daily conflict, whether internal or external, before becoming life-altering patterns.

There are no guarantees. There is much evidence-based research in journal after journal about the benefits of mindfulness meditation. Your journey is solely dependent upon you, where you are in your life, and your readiness.

Clifford L. Carter

Neutralizing Dis-Ease

Mindfulness-Based Authorized Curriculum ~ First Edition

Class One: Eye Sense

Overview

All classes begin with the same or similar format, so the participants become comfortable with the processes they are offered. The format also builds trust between the facilitator and participants. Even though each class will have new material, the structure of the class should relatively remain the same. I say this with the exception of the first two points, described in this overview of Class One: Eye Sense.

❋ As this is the first class, start with the Orientation found on page xix.

❋ Inherent benefits.

❋ Brief organizational details to follow.

Theme– Eye Sense

We start with the sensation found streaming through the eyes, as with most all living beings who have the sense of sight, it becomes the first input into the Mind from afar.

Neutralizing Dis-Ease

It was important in prehistoric times to keep one safe from predators and the unknown. In many ways, that has changed very little. Today, we do not have the predators who once roamed the earth and saw humans as food to fill their stomachs.

Today the eyes tell a different story—a story based upon past-seeing experience embedded in our MIND through one's lived environment, the people, places, and things that made up our person's world. The eyes become the filter to the teller of our story, the MIND— our story from beginning to this very day, this very moment in time.

The process of seeing can be experienced without knowing, without attachment, grasping, or aversion. In this session, we explore seeing without knowing. We learn to deeply see and understand meanings found in an object we would normally pass by.

Using the MMP practice we can open the MIND through the sense of the eye.

Time Recommendations

❀ Overview: approximately 20-30 minutes.

❀ Seeing, seeing deeply process: 45 minutes.

❀ Discussion: 15-30 minutes

❀ Homework assignment and questions: 15-20 min.

❀ Total time for first class: 2 hours.

Mindfulness Meditation Program

MINDFUL MEDITATION GUIDE

1. Choose a comfortable seated position.
2. Maintain spinal integrity.
3. Slightly tuck chin.
4. Rest hands on thighs.
5. Relax jaw.
6. Place tip of tongue behind top front teeth.
7. Close eyes or leave them slightly open.

FOCUS ON THE BREATH AS IT FLOWS IN & OUT OF THE BODY

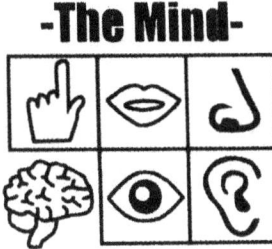

-The Mind-

BECOME AWARE OF SENSATIONS INSIDE & OUTSIDE THE BODY

✻ Give instructions about MMP practice using the guide.

✻ Questions and answers.

MINDFULNESS PROCESS

❋ Start with MMP practice.

❋ Invite participants to close their eyes, if they have not already done so.

❋ Place an object in plain sight by all participants.

❋ Invite participants to open their eyes and view the object for a few moments and then close eyes after instructed to do so, focusing on the breath and observing the object in the MIND without seeing.

❋ Give some time to be with the object in the MIND through the EYE SENSE.

❋ Invite the participants to open their eyes and view the object again. Encourage participants to look deeper—see what might not have been seen the first time.

❋ Close eyes again and bring object into the MIND while focusing on the breath and examine the object without judgment—without rightness or wrongness, but with a questioning, open MIND.

❋ Again, give some time to be with the object placed in the MIND through the EYE SENSE.

❋ Invite participants to open eyes if they are ready, and come back to the space by subtle body engaging movement.

❋ Go around the room and encourage each person to share their experience with the process.

❋ Questions and answers about MMP practice or process.

Between class practice

❋ Encourage participants to maintain a daily sitting practice using MMP's *Mindful Meditation Guide* provided.

❋ Encourage participants to see, deeply see their surrounding through a questioning Mind—a Mind free from right or wrong, good or bad.

❋ Pair the sitting practice with the Eye Sense process as much as they can. Invite them to become aware if their perceptions about their world, or the world around them, shift—even for a moment, to a more expansive questioning, observing state.

Take Away

When observing the world, our world through the Eye Sense from a questioning Mind, we then open our experience and invite all other possibilities into our daily life. We become less and less bound by past influences that paved the way to present circumstance.

Eye Sense is the first step in *letting go* of the limiting possibilities that have brought us to *now*. The new way of seeing is the first step in endless opportunity. We are beginning to learn who we really are, not by arming but disarming the Mind.

Congratulations on completing your first class. My hope is to provoke change in the most subtle way. The dam leaks before it breaks. Then, we rebuild—Better, stronger, faster, smarter.

Mindfulness Meditation Program

Notes

Neutralizing Dis-Ease

Mindfulness-Based Authorized Curriculum ~ First Edition

Class Two: Ear Sense

Theme– Ear Sense

The quality of sound vibrations experienced from our surroundings offers a unique opportunity of hearing all capable possibilities in our arena. That can be enhanced by the MMP practice. Engaging in sound with a mind positioned on questioning our experience enables us to bring about an unique new mindful-centered approach to our world.

Opening one's Mind through the Ear Sense in a way that embodies all possibilities allows those generated from our past knowing to fall away.

Past experience from all senses, including the Ear Sense, bring us to the very place we are in the moment. Voice structure, tone, inflection—even without word—are interpreted by the Mind to form a perception of safe, neutral, or unsafe. Taking time to unravel the structures, tones, inflections is a process of acceptance and *letting go* of old belief systems that charged our person from the first moment a sound traveled through the body (not just the ears). I am suggesting that even the vibration on the outer layer of one's self can be affected by sound in a profound way.

Neutralizing Dis-Ease

We explore hearing and sound vibration, along with the way in which it has connected and sometimes chained us to our past—negative, neutral, or positive experience. We then, with a questioning exploring MIND develop new pathways of hearing and even feeling vibrations.

Time Recommendations

❋ Overview: approximately 20-30 minutes.

❋ Hearing, hearing deeply process: 45 minutes.

❋ Discussion: 15-30 minutes.

❋ Homework assignment and questions: 15-20 min.

❋ Total time for class: 1 hour.

MINDFULNESS MEDITATION PROGRAM

MINDFUL MEDITATION GUIDE

1. Choose a comfortable seated position.
2. Maintain spinal integrity.
3. Slightly tuck chin.
4. Rest hands on thighs.
5. Relax jaw.
6. Place tip of tongue behind top front teeth.
7. Close eyes or leave them slightly open.

FOCUS ON THE BREATH AS IT FLOWS IN & OUT OF THE BODY

BECOME AWARE OF SENSATIONS INSIDE & OUTSIDE THE BODY

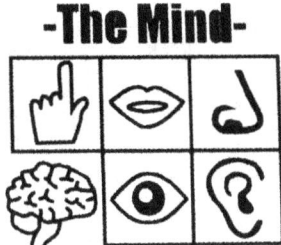

❋ Give instructions about MMP practice using the guide.

❋ Questions and answers.

Mindfulness Process

✸ Start with MMP practice.

✸ Invite participants to close their eyes, if they have not already done so.

✸ Choose a type of sound you wish to explore. The choice might be from a music CD or an unusual instrument or even a sound-making object. I encourage you to choose something you hope will be unusual enough the participants easily move to a questioning MIND.

✸ Invite participants to immerse themselves in the sound, including any sense of the vibration that might be happening—exploring as many facets of the experience they can without naming or judging what is being heard.

✸ Allow the participants time to fully embrace the experience through an unknowing, questioning MIND.

✸ Invite participants to open eyes if they are ready and come back to the space by subtle body engaging movement.

✸ Go around the room, encourage each persons to share their experience with the EAR SENSE process.

✸ Questions and answers about MMP practice or process.

Between class practice

✸ Encourage participants to maintain a daily sitting practice using MMP's *Mindful Meditation Guide* provided.

✳ Encourage participants to hear and feel hearing happening on the body.

✳ Encourage participants to experience hearing for the first time as much as possible—with a MIND free from right or wrong, good or bad.

✳ Pair the sitting practice with the EAR SENSE as much as they can, and invite them to become aware if their perceptions about their world, or the world around them, shift—even for a moment, to a more expansive, questioning, observing state.

TAKE AWAY

Hearing. What is hearing but soft, medium, or strong vibration floating onto and into the body though the human surface and ear? EAR SENSE is a useful tool that gets us from point A to point B, by some spoken direction or outside hearing that channels us down a particular road or path.

The channel was formed by our past influences and obstacles we've encountered along the way, bringing us to this point in our life. Some influences seem to be encouraging one to continue. Others seem to position in front of, beside, or even behind us—like a water stream, filled with outcropping rock faces and downed tree branches, filtering the water on an uncertain path.

The transformational part is the same with all senses—that is, to hear what has yet to be heard by you.

Feel the sound that has not yet landed on the flesh of your being. Change, renegotiate the known sound to the unknown, from the strong to weak, and weak to strong, eventually settling in the middle—showing up as neutral.

With questioning MIND, open expansive MIND, we explore and examine every facet of the EAR SENSE experience when encouraged.

MINDFULNESS MEDITATION PROGRAM

Notes

> "Trust your body. Question your brain."
>
> — Clifford L. Carter

Neutralizing Dis-Ease

MINDFULNESS-BASED AUTHORIZED CURRICULUM ~ FIRST EDITION

Class Three: Nose Sense

Theme– Nose Sense

SMELL IS A POWERFUL TOOL in many ways—some of which we do not fully understand. From the scent of breakfast in the morning traveling into the MIND space, the reaction as hunger, like-dislike, memories bound to childhood, or an outing with a best friend gone by.

For me, a subtle scent of a certain fragrance gives me the ability to float far, far away from the debilitating experience and into a dissociative land—free from pain and suffering. Today, after forty years, when I smell that scent again, I visit the memory of water splashing against the shoreline. The warm sun on my face, and the feeling of cool blades of grass under my feet arises. The memory as I know what happened that very day, trapped in my body, waiting for *smell* to release yet again and again, never to fully escape my being. I have a knowing and a body sensation, but the act of assault is no longer present. Only the floating away to another land, another time and space, free from suffering exists today.

As I use MMP when these sensations trigger an experience from my past, I am able to calmly explore the happenings, be with the experience, accept the experience as the past, and move on to the next sensation that arises. The process of becoming aware, being with, accept, and move on to another sensation happens in the MIND. What follows is the real magic.

When acceptance happens in the MIND, the body follows by *letting go*. The process of Sensation, Thought, Action, Acceptance, and Letting Go, when practiced, becomes the first step in recognizing nothing is permanent, things come and things go.

When we trap a sense in the body and feed the sense, it becomes a part of who we believe ourselves to be—further solidifying these thought by actions of pulling validating experiences into our consciousness.

TIME RECOMMENDATIONS

* Overview: approximately 20-30 minutes.
* Smelling, smelling deeply process: 45 minutes.
* Discussion: 15-30 minutes.
* Homework assignment and questions: 15-20 min.
* Total time for class: 1 hour.

Mindfulness Meditation Program

MINDFUL MEDITATION GUIDE

1. Choose a comfortable seated position.
2. Maintain spinal integrity.
3. Slightly tuck chin.
4. Rest hands on thighs.
5. Relax jaw.
6. Place tip of tongue behind top front teeth.
7. Close eyes or leave them slightly open.

FOCUS ON THE BREATH AS IT FLOWS IN & OUT OF THE BODY

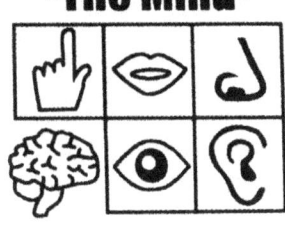

BECOME AWARE OF SENSATIONS INSIDE & OUTSIDE THE BODY

❋ Give instructions about MMP practice using the guide.

❋ Questions and answers.

Mindfulness Process

❋ Start with MMP practice.

❋ Invite participants to close their eyes, if they have not already done so.

❋ Choose a scent that is pleasant, not overwhelming. And if possible, a scent that is not so common to the nose.

❋ As participants sit with their eyes closed, either with a diffuser or simply going around the room with a cotton ball with a dab of scent on it, allow the participants to fully experience their NOSE SENSE.

❋ Do not stop moving around the room, so the scent comes and goes from subtle to a little more intense.

❋ Encourage participants to focus on the breath and bring into the MIND space the scent you have provided.

❋ Invite them to smell fully and completely. See if they can open their MIND to the NOSE SENSE experience without judging right or wrong, good or bad.

❋ Invite participants to open eyes if they are ready, and come back to the space by subtle body engaging movement.

❋ Go around the room, encouraging each person to share their experience with the NOSE SENSE process.

❋ Questions and answers about MMP practice or process.

Between class practice

❋ Encourage participants to maintain a daily sitting practice using MMP's *Mindful Meditation Guide* provided.

❋ Encourage participants to fully smell everything.

❋ Encourage participants to experience smells for the first time as much as possible, with a MIND free from right or wrong, good or bad.

❋ Pair the sitting practice with the NOSE SENSE process as much as they can, and invite them to become aware if their perceptions about their world, or the world around them, shift—even for a moment, to a more expansive, questioning, observing state.

Take Away

Smelling. As I breathe in and breathe out, the sensation of smell encourages and discourages action. The space between act and non-act is neutral. Accepting what is in the moment and *letting go* of the notions, I am, or I am not.

The memory of my great aunt's kitchen brimming with the aroma of freshly picked peaches from the orchard just outside and the morning's fresh cream from the Jersey milk cow. How sweet that fills my being. Compared with the scent of cologne from a trauma experience—both have the nature of clinging.

One is pulling toward and the other is pushing away. The energies are the same and can lead us to unhappiness. It's the space between the neutral space that allows one to explore and find new hidden meanings in our world. The open accepting and *letting go*—not of the experience but letting go of the hold it has.

The defining properties placed on the past informs our future with every breath in and out. That is the powerful sense of smell. It's up to us to encourage the scent and allow the exploration of the scent, *letting go* of the defining hold it has on us. It enables a sense of peace and calm to fill the MIND with the knowing—We are alive and free to experience unencumbered joy.

MINDFULNESS MEDITATION PROGRAM

Notes

_____

_____

_____

_____

_____

_____

_____

_____

_____

_____

_____

Neutralizing Dis-Ease

MINDFULNESS-BASED AUTHORIZED CURRICULUM ~ FIRST EDITION

Class Four: Taste Sense

Theme– Taste Sense

Every single bite taken either connects us to a past experience held over in the MIND or becomes a challenging thought full of exploration. It is our choice how we perceive the taste that lands on the tongue; either sweet, sour, bitter, mild, or salty. The components that make up a taste experience are filled with texture, crunch, warm, cool, and so many more.

The sensations in TASTE SENSE can bring us to a place far from now, steeped in the past—whether good, bad, or neutral.

Living in Bermuda for two years, some flavors were notable and others were as foreign as that small island in the Atlantic. Longing for some memory of *home*, I found a quiet little restaurant, patronized by mostly locals, that served my hometown favorites—hamburger, French fries, and a coke. I ate there one time a week and savored the flavors, closing my eyes and then reopening them, imagining I was far away from that place and back to a time of comfort and calm—away from the lonely, self-reliant call that has solidified my being in this world.

I suddenly am no longer alone in my thoughts in the little diner filled with others enjoying bacon, eggs, burgers, and fries.

As some tastes take us to a time and place of comfort, other tastes have a pulling quality and can become clinging, craving, grasping, and averting. Tasting unknown flavors can have a grasping, neutral, or averting affect. It is dependent on our openness and accepting TASTE SENSE that can far surpass our own walled pallet.

As I use MMP practice when these sensations trigger an experience from my past, I am able to calmly explore the happenings, be with the experience, accept the experience as the past, and move on to the next sensation that arises. The process of becoming aware, be with, accept, and move on to another sensation happens in the Mind. What follows is the real magic.

When acceptance happens in the Mind, the body follows by *letting go*. The process of Sensation, Thought, Action, Acceptance, Letting Go when practiced, becomes the first step in recognizing nothing is permanent–things come and things go. When we trap a sense in the body and feed that sense, it becomes a part of who we believe ourselves to be–further solidifying the thought by actions of pulling validating experiences into our consciousness.

Time Recommendations

- Overview: approximately 20-30 minutes.
- Tasting, tasting deeply process: 45 minutes.
- Discussion: 15-30 minutes.

* Homework assignment and questions: 15-20 min.
* Total time for class: 1 hour.

MINDFULNESS MEDITATION PROGRAM

MINDFUL MEDITATION GUIDE

1. Choose a comfortable seated position.
2. Maintain spinal integrity.
3. Slightly tuck chin.
4. Rest hands on thighs.
5. Relax jaw.
6. Place tip of tongue behind top front teeth.
7. Close eyes or leave them slightly open.

FOCUS ON THE BREATH AS IT FLOWS IN & OUT OF THE BODY

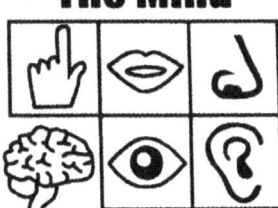

-The Mind-

BECOME AWARE OF SENSATIONS INSIDE & OUTSIDE THE BODY

❈ Give instructions about MMP practice using the guide.

❈ Questions and answers.

MINDFULNESS PROCESS

❈ Start with MMP practice.

❈ Invite participants to close their eyes, if they have not already done so.

❈ Choose an unexpected taste, providing texture with sweet, sour, and salty that can challenge the TASTE SENSE and the MIND to have an internal dialogue with what is being experienced.

❈ As participants sit with their eyes closed, walk around, offering each person to take the object and put into their mouth. While experiencing the TASTE SENSE as if they are analyzing every facet, allow the participants to fully experience taste.

❈ Encourage participants to focus on the breath and bring into the MIND space the taste you have provided.

❈ Taste fully and completely. Ask them to see if they can open the MIND to the experience without judging right or wrong, good or bad.

❈ Invite participants to open eyes if they are ready and come back to the space by subtle body engaging movement.

❈ Go around the room, encouraging each person to share their TASTE SENSE experience with the process.

❈ Questions and answers about MMP practice or process.

BETWEEN CLASS PRACTICE

❉ Encourage participants to maintain a daily sitting practice using MMP's *Mindful Meditation Guide* provided.

❉ Encourage participants to fully taste everything.

❉ Encourage participants to experience TASTE SENSE for the first time as much as possible, with a MIND free from right or wrong, good or bad.

❉ Pair the sitting practice with the tasting process as much as they can and invite them become aware if their perceptions about their world, or the world around them, shift—even for a moment, to a more expansive, questioning, observing state.

TAKE AWAY

Taste is a transformational sense and has the ability to take us to the past, present, and dreaming of the future. All can have the quality of clinging, craving, grasping, or aversion. If we taste with the wonder of a child's mind and expansively explore the experience, we can question all facets of the experience—exploration free from judgment, free from right, wrong, good, or bad. In the experience of acceptance real transformation occurs—transformation free from the tethers of a past that clings to the *who we have become* in the present and *who we will be* in our future.

How has taste become so powerful to determine our experience—past, present, and future? It is the *who we have become*, based on all the senses plus the THINKING MIND that solidifies our being and further informs our future. The way out of the cycle for grasping and aversion becomes accepting what is—without holding on to the past and hopes for the future.

MMP practice of focusing on the breath and becoming aware of sensation: Be with sensation, accept sensation, and move on to the next sensation that arises. That enables us to explore a transformational destination. Acceptance is in the MIND space and then allows the body to let go of any grasping or aversion that might be happening in the moment. The open, accepting MIND facilitates a present and future consciousness.

MINDFULNESS MEDITATION PROGRAM

Notes

_____

_____

_____

_____

_____

_____

_____

_____

_____

Neutralizing Dis-Ease

Mindfulness-Based Authorized Curriculum ~ First Edition

Class Five: Touch Sense

Theme– Touch Sense

THE TOUCH OF A COOL glass in your hand, the weight and the texture on your lips provide knowledge placed into the MIND space. Warmth of a fire on our skin and the sensation of our arm hair standing straight up when chilled. Tension, tightness, stabbing, or throbbing are just a few experiences in the body, providing the sense of touch to our MIND.

The physical touch from another human or the subtle vibrations happening when we are close in proximity to someone can have profound consequence in solidifying one's experience. The touch of a pet (dog, cat, snake, fish, or bird) can calm the nervous system or ramp it up, depending on your perception placed on the touch.

Feeling the outer layer of an animal through the palm of our hand sends information to the MIND that quickly discerns how we'll think and feel. For some, the sight of a small dog becomes fearful as having a past encounter of being chased or even bitten. Both of which have the qualities of TOUCH SENSE, along with other senses.

As I use MMP practice when these sensations trigger an experience from my past, I am able to calmly explore the happenings, be with the experience, accept the experience as the past, and move on to the next sensation that arises.

The process of becoming aware, be with, accept and move on to another sensation happens in the MIND and what follows is the real magic. When acceptance happens in the MIND, the body follows by *letting go*.

The process of Sensation, Thought, Action, Acceptance, Letting go, when practiced, becomes the first step in recognizing nothing is permanent—things come and things go. When we trap a sense in the body and feed the sense, it becomes a part of who we believe ourselves to be—further solidifying the thought by pulling validating experiences into our consciousness.

TIME RECOMMENDATIONS

* Overview: approximately 20-30 minutes.
* Touching, touching deeply process: 45 minutes.
* Discussion: 15-30 minutes.
* Homework assignment and questions: 15-20 min.
* Total time for class: 1 hour.

Mindfulness Meditation Program

MINDFUL MEDITATION GUIDE

1. Choose a comfortable seated position.
2. Maintain spinal integrity.
3. Slightly tuck chin.
4. Rest hands on thighs.
5. Relax jaw.
6. Place tip of tongue behind top front teeth.
7. Close eyes or leave them slightly open.

FOCUS
ON THE BREATH
AS IT FLOWS IN & OUT
OF THE BODY

-The Mind-

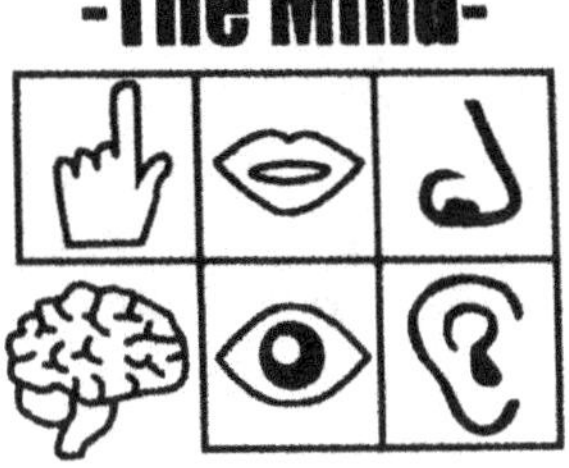

BECOME AWARE
OF SENSATIONS INSIDE
& OUTSIDE THE BODY

❋ Give instructions about MMP practice using the guide.

❋ Questions and answers.

MINDFULNESS PROCESS

❋ Start with MMP practice.

❋ Invite participants to close their eyes, if they have not already done so.

❋ Choose an unexpected object, as many differing as possible, that can challenge the MIND to have an internal dialogue with what is happening.

❋ As participants sit with their eyes closed, walk around offering each person to take the object as if they are analyzing every facet. Allow the participants to fully experience touch.

❋ Encourage participants to focus on the breath and bring into the MIND space the TOUCH SENSE you have provided.

❋ Touch fully and completely. See if they can open their MIND to the experience without judging right or wrong, good or bad.

❋ Invite participants to open eyes, if they are ready and come back to the space by subtle body engaging movement.

❋ Go around the room, encouraging each person to share their experience with the TOUCH SENSE process.

❋ Questions and answers about MMP practice or process.

BETWEEN CLASS PRACTICE

❋ Encourage participants to maintain a daily sitting practice using MMP's *Mindful Meditation Guide* provided.

✱ Encourage participants to fully touch.

✱ Encourage participants to experience TOUCH SENSE for the first time as much as possible, with a MIND free from right or wrong, good or bad.

✱ Pair the sitting practice with the touch process as much as they can, and become aware if their perceptions about their world, or the world around them, shift—even for a moment, to a more expansive, questioning, observing state.

TAKE AWAY

Whether with hands or feet, explore the external quality of TOUCH SENSE as if it is the first exploration of an object or foot on a well-traveled path. Touch sensation lives both inside and out, as hair swaying back and forth on skin or the feeling of a breeze that facilitates the action. We can feel through the sense of touch even without being touched or actually touching anything. The body exploration through TOUCH SENSE arises as a feeling but is rooted in the texture of responding to by pleasure, pain, good, and bad.

Simply allow and explore the subtle and not so subtle feelings associated with touch, past-informed present as well as future through our TOUCH SENSE.

The way out of the cycle of grasping and aversion becomes accepting what is. Without holding on to the past and hope for the future, practice MMP focusing on the breath and becoming aware of sensation. Being with sensation, accepting sensation, and moving on to the next sensation that arises enables us to explore a transformational destination. The acceptance piece is in the MIND space and then allows the body to let go of any grasping or aversion that might be happening in the moment. The open, accepting MIND facilitates a present and future consciousness.

MINDFULNESS MEDITATION PROGRAM

Notes

"There are both selfish and selfless individuals in this world. One cannot be the other."

Clifford L Carter

Neutralizing Dis-Ease

Mindfulness-Based Authorized Curriculum ~ First Edition

Class Six: Thinking Mind

Theme– Thinking Mind

THE THINKING MIND—NOT TO BE confused with the MIND space that has vast experience in creating a safe world or even unsafe world (depending on the *who we have become* and the way we see ourselves, along with the way we'd like others to see us) has the ability of generating thought without stimulus.

The intrusive thought that seemingly comes out of nowhere is not influenced by anything at all. Quite the contrary. Those thoughts are influenced by past experiences we allow to solidify by believing "This is who I am". The belief is further kept solid by creating experiences that facilitate that belief in self. The MIND, when challenged by new thought, and questioning our THINKING MIND enables us to rewrite our future in the present by thoughts that are not held to past narrow thinking.

As I use MMP practice when those sensations trigger an experience from my past, I am able to calmly explore the happenings, be with the experience, accept the experience as the past, and move on to the next sensation that arises.

The process of becoming aware, be with, accept, and move on to another sensation happens in the MIND and what follows is the real magic. When acceptance happens in the MIND, the body follows by *letting go*.

The process of Sensation, Thought, Action, Acceptance, Letting go, when practiced, becomes the first step in recognizing nothing is permanent—things come and things go. When we trap a sense in the body and feed the sense, it becomes a part of who we believe ourselves to be—further solidifying the thought by actions of pulling validating experiences into our consciousness.

TIME RECOMMENDATIONS

* Overview: approximately 20-30 minutes.
* Thinking, thinking deeply process: 45 minutes.
* Discussion: 15-30 minutes.
* Homework assignment and questions: 15-20 min.
* Total time for class: 1 hour.

Mindfulness Meditation Program

MINDFUL MEDITATION GUIDE

1. Choose a comfortable seated position.
2. Maintain spinal integrity.
3. Slightly tuck chin.
4. Rest hands on thighs.
5. Relax jaw.
6. Place tip of tongue behind top front teeth.
7. Close eyes or leave them slightly open.

FOCUS ON THE BREATH AS IT FLOWS IN & OUT OF THE BODY

BECOME AWARE OF SENSATIONS INSIDE & OUTSIDE THE BODY

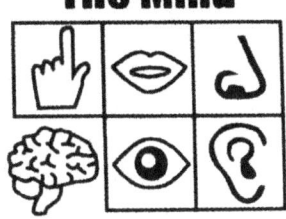

❊ Give instructions about MMP practice, using the guide.

❊ Questions and answer.

Mindfulness Process

❋ Start with MMP practice.

❋ Invite participants to close their eyes, if they have not already done so.

❋ Encourage participants to become aware of thoughts.

❋ As participants sit with their eyes closed, reinforce the idea that thoughts come and thoughts go. Just as clouds float though the sky, allow thoughts to enter and exit the MIND.

❋ Encourage participants to focus on the breath and bring into the MIND space every arising thought.

❋ Be with the THINKING MIND, accept the thought and move on to another thought.

❋ Think each thought fully and completely. See if they can open their MIND to the experience without judging right or wrong, good or bad.

❋ Invite participants to open their eyes if they are ready and come back to the space by subtle body engaging movement.

❋ Go around the room, encouraging each person to share their experience with the process.

❋ Questions and answers about MMP practice or process.

Between class practice

❋ Encourage participants to maintain a daily sitting practice using MMP's *Mindful Meditation Guide* provided.

✺ Encourage participants to fully explore their THINKING MIND.

✺ Encourage participants to experience thought as if it were a new thought without origin—not belonging to them—simply a thought with a MIND free from right or wrong, good or bad.

✺ Pair the sitting practice with the thinking process as much as they can, and invite them to become aware if their perceptions about their world, or the world around them, shift—even for a moment, to a more expansive, questioning, observing state.

TAKE AWAY

Our thoughts are not our own. More simply, they are who we have become based on all the perceptions from one's past surrounding, rolled up into a stream of conscious thought that may or may not have bearing on what is happening in the moment.

Allowing thoughts to come and thoughts to go enables us to challenge the beliefs about our self and the world around us. Thinking, and intrusive thoughts seemingly coming from nowhere, have an origin deep inside that has the ability to keep one safe or stuck in the same cycles of pain and suffering. The only way to interrupt the THINKING MIND is accepting and allowing the thought to come and to go.

The way out of the cycle of grasping and aversion becomes accepting what is, without holding on to the past or hopes for the future, is the MMP practice of focusing on the breath and becoming aware of sensation. Being with sensation, accepting sensation, and moving on to the next sensation that arises enables us to explore a transformational destination. The acceptance piece is in the MIND space, and then allows the body to let go of any grasping or aversion that might be happening in the moment. The open accepting MIND facilitates a present and future consciousness.

MINDFULNESS MEDITATION PROGRAM

Notes

"Overthinking is connecting with past experiences in an attempt to feel safe and validated in the present."

Clifford L. Carter

Neutralizing Dis-Ease

MINDFULNESS-BASED AUTHORIZED CURRICULUM ~ FIRST EDITION

Class Seven: The Mind

Theme— The Mind

WE CAN THINK OF THE MIND as a space, a catalog of all the past knowledge and experiences we have encountered in our lifetime—a library informed by yes-no, right-wrong, safe-unsafe. When our senses fire off, the information travels to the MIND, and that's where we form an opinion based on sensory input. That space decides what measures will be taken to counter if necessary, accept, or simply let go of the message being transmitted.

The library of ours, based on what I call *Environmental Pollutants*, has an endless capacity for change. However the MIND is very reluctant to change because the very idea of change can be frightening. Change can challenge the knowledge that has kept one feeling safe and secure. The process of challenging the beliefs stored in the MIND starts with analyzing and carefully deciding if the past experience still has merit in our life today.

As I use MMP practice when these sensations trigger an experience from my past, I am able to calmly explore the happenings, be with the experience, accept the experience as the past, and move on to the next sensation that arises. The process of becoming aware, be with, accept, and move on to another sensation happens in the MIND. What follows is the real magic. When acceptance happens in the MIND, the body follows by *letting go*—the process of Sensation, Thought, Action, Acceptance, Letting go.

TIME RECOMMENDATIONS

✻ Overview: approximately 20-30 minutes.

✻ Sensing, sensing deeply process: 45 minutes.

✻ Discussion: 15-30 minutes.

✻ Homework assignment and questions: 15-20 min.

✻ Total time for class: 1 hour.

Mindfulness Meditation Program

MINDFUL MEDITATION GUIDE

1. Choose a comfortable seated position.
2. Maintain spinal integrity.
3. Slightly tuck chin.
4. Rest hands on thighs.
5. Relax jaw.
6. Place tip of tongue behind top front teeth.
7. Close eyes or leave them slightly open.

FOCUS ON THE BREATH AS IT FLOWS IN & OUT OF THE BODY

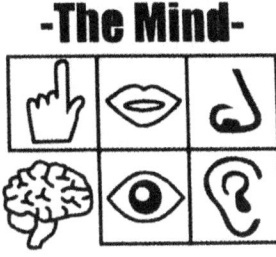
-The Mind-

BECOME AWARE OF SENSATIONS INSIDE & OUTSIDE THE BODY

✵ Give instructions about MMP practice using the guide.

✵ Questions and answers.

Mindfulness Process

❋ Start with MMP practice.

❋ Invite participants to close their eyes, if they have not already done so.

❋ Encourage participants to become aware of all senses.

❋ Encourage participants to focus on the breath and bring into the MIND space every sensation that arises.

❋ Be with the sensation, accept sensation, and move on to the next sensation that arises.

❋ Experience each sense fully and completely. See if they can open their MIND to the experience without judging right or wrong, good or bad.

❋ Invite participants to open eyes if they are ready and come back to the space by subtle body engaging movement.

❋ Go around the room, encouraging each person to share their experience with the process.

❋ Questions and answers about MMP practice or process.

Between class practice

❋ Encourage participants to maintain a daily sitting practice using MMP's *Mindful Meditation Guide* provided.

❋ Encourage participants to fully explore all sensations.

✸ Encourage participants to experience each sense as if it were a new sense without origin, not belonging to them, simply a sense with a MIND free from right or wrong, good or bad.

✸ Pair the sitting practice with the sensing process as much as they can and invite them to become aware if their perceptions about their world, or the world around them, shift—even for a moment, to a more expansive questioning, observing state.

TAKE AWAY

The MIND library continuously catalogs every sensation placed there. The rows and rows and rows of information are filed into categories (safe-neutral-unsafe). Once the incoming message is placed in one of those areas, we either process the message or simply file the message and move on to the next arriving sense.

If the message can be processed as neutral, there becomes no grasping or aversion. It allows the MIND to expand and explore the unknown. However, if the message is filed as safe or unsafe, it becomes a validation steeped in past knowing of our being and further informs our future experience.

The goal is to encourage the MIND to encounter experience as neutral, and question whether or not it's the *who you have become* or simply just another message to process—a message that has no attachment to the *who you truly are*—a freeing example of the *who you can become*.

The way out of the cycle of grasping and aversion becomes accepting what is. Without holding on to the past or hopes for the future, MMP practice of focusing on the breath and becoming aware of sensation, be with sensation, accept sensation, and move on to the next sensation that arises enables us to explore a transformational destination.

The acceptance piece is in the MIND space and allows the body to let go of any grasping or aversion that might be happening in the moment. The open and accepting MIND facilitates a present and future consciousness.

MINDFULNESS MEDITATION PROGRAM

Notes

_____

_____

_____

_____

_____

_____

_____

_____

_____

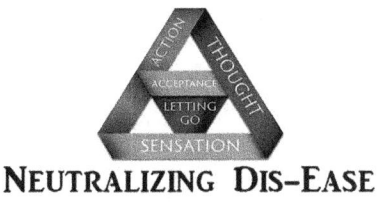

Neutralizing Dis-Ease

Mindfulness-Based Authorized Curriculum ~ First Edition

Class Eight: Action

Theme– Action

Acting upon a thought placed in the Mind through our senses becomes the way all creatures operate—whether the six senses are present or some senses are strengthened by the loss of another sense.

Action and non-action become a choice, determined by our past, facilitated by the idea of *who we are*. Right-wrong, good-bad is acted out by clinging to a time long gone. It has little to do with the here and now. Aversion to an act or grasping action seemingly forced by the Mind makes the *who we are* more and more solid by acting with all sensations simultaneously firing. Action is further facilitated by the Mind seeing through each sense, calculating the next response. It happens so quickly the response becomes clouded with thousands of past actions responding in the same or similar fashion that further influences present with past.

As I use MMP practice when these sensations trigger an experience from my past, I am able to calmly explore the happenings, be with the experience, accept the experience as the past, and move on to the next sensation that arises.

Neutralizing Dis-Ease

The process of becoming aware, be with, accept and move on to another sensation happens in the MIND. What follows is the real magic.

When acceptance happens in the MIND, the body follows by *letting go*. This is the process of Sensation, Thought, Action, Acceptance, Letting go.

Time Recommendations

❋ Overview: approximately 20-30 minutes.

❋ Sensing, sensing deeply process: 45 minutes.

❋ Discussion: 15-30 minutes.

❋ Homework assignment and questions: 15-20 min.

❋ Total time for class: 1 hour.

Mindfulness Meditation Program

MINDFUL MEDITATION GUIDE

1. Choose a comfortable seated position.
2. Maintain spinal integrity.
3. Slightly tuck chin.
4. Rest hands on thighs.
5. Relax jaw.
6. Place tip of tongue behind top front teeth.
7. Close eyes or leave them slightly open.

FOCUS ON THE BREATH AS IT FLOWS IN & OUT OF THE BODY

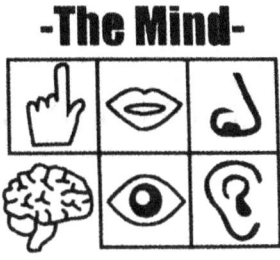

-The Mind-

BECOME AWARE OF SENSATIONS INSIDE & OUTSIDE THE BODY

❋ Give instructions about MMP practice using the guide.

❋ Questions and answers.

MINDFULNESS PROCESS

❋ Start with MMP practice.

❋ Invite participants to close their eyes, if they have not already done so.

❋ Encourage participants to become aware of thoughts inside and outside their body.

❋ Encourage participants to focus on the breath and bring into the MIND space all six senses arising that lead to ACTION.

❋ Be aware the thought of itching encourages one to scratch. See what happens when the action of scratching an itch is circumvented by moving our attention to another sensation. Come back to the itch to see if it still persists, or if the qualities of the itch have changed at all.

❋ Be with the sensation, accept sensation, and move on to another arising sensation.

❋ Think each act or non-act fully and completely. Open the MIND to the experience without judging right or wrong, good or bad, pleasure or pain.

❋ Invite participants to open their eyes if they are ready and come back to the space by subtle body engaging movement.

❋ Go around the room, encouraging each person to share their experience with the process.

❋ Questions and answers about MMP practice or process.

BETWEEN CLASS PRACTICE

❋ Encourage participants to maintain a daily sitting practice using MMP's *Mindful Meditation Guide* provided.

❋ Encourage participants to fully explore their sensations that lead to action.

❋ Encourage participants to experience sensation without action as if it were a new experience without origin, not belonging to them—simply a thought with a MIND free from right or wrong, good or bad, pleasure or pain.

❋ Pair the sitting practice with the ACTION process as much as they can and invite them to become aware if their perceptions about their world, or the world around them, shift—even for a moment, to a more expansive, questioning, observing state.

TAKE AWAY

ACTION and non-action carry the same amount of energy as grasping and aversion do. When we decide to act or not act on a thing, we become controlled by the thing. The way of *letting go* is accepting what is happening with a neutral MIND. That enables us to explore thought, with or without ACTION.

A new action forms from non-triggering influences based on a new and different way of acting out beliefs and non-beliefs that previously led us to a stuck and closed MIND. An open, accepting MIND leads to transformation through questioning.

The way out of the cycle of grasping and aversion becomes accepting what is, without holding on to the past or hopes for the future. MMP practice of focusing on the breath and becoming aware of sensation, be with sensation, accept sensation, and move on to the next sensation that arises, enables us to explore a transformational destination.

The acceptance piece is in the MIND space and then allows the body to let go of any grasping or aversion that might be happening in the moment. The open, accepting MIND facilitates a present and future consciousness.

MINDFULNESS MEDITATION PROGRAM

Notes

_____

_____

_____

_____

_____

_____

_____

_____

"Accepting a thing opens us to explore without judgment. Judgment is based on past experience solidified by clinging. Acceptance allows one to let go. When we let go, things move freely through us. Without attachment."

Clifford L. Carter

Neutralizing Dis-Ease

Mindfulness-Based Authorized Curriculum ~ First Edition

Class Nine: Acceptance

Theme– Acceptance

When I think of acceptance, the *twelve step program* is the first thing that comes to mind. "Grant me the serenity to accept the things I cannot change, the courage to change the things I can, and the wisdom to know the difference" has been used for many years to manage life challenges through a process of acceptance.

For our purposes, this does not mean we turn our back on challenges, rather the opposite. We embrace challenges as they are in the moment, knowing in the next moment of understanding our challenge will certainly change.

Something as simple as sitting on a cushion meditating with thoughts or body tensions becomes challenging. The idea is to be with, accept, and move on to another arising sensation. Then going back to the challenging sensation, exploring and recognizing the change that has occurred. It is the mindful process of exploring sensation with an open, expansive mind—recognizing sensations come and sensations go, becoming impermanent parts of our being.

For our purposes, challenges are not defined as bad or good, rather simply a sensation in the moment. As grasping and aversion can lead to unhappiness. Focusing on and naming a pleasurable sensation has the same quality as a painful sensation, in the sense we cling to our understanding as being right or wrong. The process of acceptance leads to a physical *letting go*.

As I use MMP practice when these sensations trigger an experience from my past, I am able to calmly explore the happenings, be with the experience, accept the experience as the past, and move on to the next sensation that arises. The process of becoming aware, be with, accept, and move on to another sensation happens in the MIND. What follows is the real magic.

When acceptance happens in the MIND, the body follows by *letting go*. This is the process of Sensation, Thought, Action, Acceptance, Letting go.

TIME RECOMMENDATIONS

- ❋ Overview: approximately 20-30 minutes.
- ❋ Sensing, sensing deeply process: 45 minutes.
- ❋ Discussion: 15-30 minutes.
- ❋ Homework assignment and questions: 15-20 min.
- ❋ Total time for class: 1 hour.

Mindfulness Meditation Program

MINDFUL MEDITATION GUIDE

1. Choose a comfortable seated position.
2. Maintain spinal integrity.
3. Slightly tuck chin.
4. Rest hands on thighs.
5. Relax jaw.
6. Place tip of tongue behind top front teeth.
7. Close eyes or leave them slightly open.

FOCUS ON THE BREATH AS IT FLOWS IN & OUT OF THE BODY

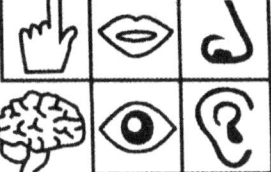

BECOME AWARE OF SENSATIONS INSIDE & OUTSIDE THE BODY

✺ Give instructions about MMP practice using the guide.

✺ Questions and answers.

MINDFULNESS PROCESS

❋ Start with MMP practice.

❋ Invite participants to close their eyes, if they have not already done so.

❋ Encourage participants to become aware of sensations inside and outside their body.

❋ Encourage participants to focus on the breath and bring into the MIND space sensations, one-by-one all six senses.

❋ Be aware the sensation happening inside and outside the body. Focus awareness on one sensation, be with, accept, and move on to another sensation. Then, return to the former sensation, noticing any change.

❋ Change in any sensory: Seeing, tasting, touching, smelling, hearing, thinking mind.

❋ Be with each sensation fully and completely. Invite them to open their mind to the experience without judging right or wrong, good or bad, pleasure or pain.

❋ Invite participants to open eyes if they are ready and come back to the space by subtle body engaging movement.

❋ Go around the room, encouraging each person to share their experience with the process.

❋ Questions and answers about MMP practice or process.

BETWEEN CLASS PRACTICE

✸ Encourage participants to maintain a daily sitting practice using MMP's *Mindful Meditation Guide* provided.

✸ Encourage participants to fully explore all six sensations.

✸ Encourage participants to experience sensations as a new sense without origin, not belonging to them, simply a sense with a MIND free from right or wrong, good or bad, pleasure or pain.

✸ Pair the sitting practice with the sensation process as much as they can and become aware if their perceptions about their world, or the world around them, shift—even for a moment, to a more expansive, questioning, observing state.

TAKE AWAY

Acceptance can be very challenging and is a process with lasting positive effects. Human beings have the capacity to feel all possible emotions and experiences. Accepting is the way through and into the endless possibilities that otherwise hold our thinking hostage to beliefs that may or may not be true for us.

When we look at a neighbor or even someone passing by on a street, or even on the nightly news, the tendency is to judge and form an opinion of the person that sometimes leads to unacceptability. As soon as we generate the feeling of unacceptability, the relationship with the person or situation begins to close.

In most cases, the reason is we have an experience with what we are sensing about the person—relationship deep inside we would like to hold down and not deal with. But, if we can look at the situation as a teaching moment—the thought comes from inside us and lives inside, only projecting our self onto another. How else would we be able to not accept another path unless some light had been shown on our own journey?

The way out of the cycle of grasping and aversion becomes accepting what is, without holding on to the past or hopes for the future. MMP practice of focusing on the breath and becoming aware of sensation, be with sensation, accept sensation, and move on to the next sensation that arises, enables us to explore a transformational destination.

The acceptance piece is in the MIND space and then allows the body to let go of any grasping or aversion that might be happening in the moment. The open, accepting MIND facilitates a present and future consciousness.

MINDFULNESS MEDITATION PROGRAM

Notes

"Always grasping outside ourselves for internal struggles seems to be backwards, but I guess it's human nature when we think we are not enough."

Clifford L Carter

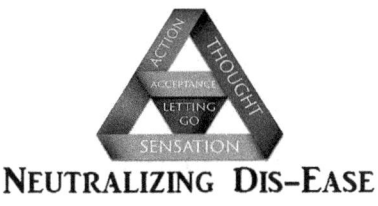

Neutralizing Dis-Ease
Mindfulness-Based Authorized Curriculum ~ First Edition

Class Ten: Letting Go

Theme– Letting Go

Holding onto a thing or feeling can become debilitating over time. Just how long do you think someone could hold a tennis ball, for instance? Tennis balls are meant to be held, so they're comfortable in the palm, even a little fuzzy to the touch. One might even enjoy holding a tennis ball for a short period. As time continues, the holding manifests into labor by tightening of the forearm, sweaty palm, shoulder pain, and racing thoughts about abandoning the senseless exercise.

All things have the same quality as the tennis ball in the sense that in the beginning the thought or sense might feel pleasurable or maybe even painful. When we finish with the sensation, we accept the outcome followed by *letting go*.

The sensation of *letting go* is a physical as well as a mental relaxation. When we become able to let go of a thing, it no longer has an effect on the *who we have become*. Rather, it leads us to our true nature. Our true nature has a light, open, transparent, and a still or calm state of being.

Neutralizing Dis-Ease

The process of mindfully *letting go* is the process of *neutralizing dis-ease*. Dis-ease is manifested by holding on to a sensation that has been triggered by the MIND as needed to facilitate change. The truth is, holding only manifests suffering in the end. Either good, bad, pleasure, or pain, holding on is the physical part of unacceptability.

As I use MMP practice when sensations trigger an experience from my past, I am able to calmly explore the happenings, be with the experience, accept the experience as the past, and move on to the next sensation that arises. The process of becoming aware, being with, accept, and move on to another sensation happens in the MIND. What follows is the real magic.

When acceptance happens in the MIND the body follows by *letting go*. This process: Sensation, Thought, Action, Acceptance, Letting go.

Time Recommendations

* Overview: approximately 20-30 minutes.
* Sensing, sensing deeply process: 45 minutes.
* Discussion: 15-30 minutes.
* Homework assignment and questions: 15-20 min.
* Total time for class: 1 hour.

MINDFULNESS MEDITATION PROGRAM

MINDFUL MEDITATION GUIDE

1. Choose a comfortable seated position.
2. Maintain spinal integrity.
3. Slightly tuck chin.
4. Rest hands on thighs.
5. Relax jaw.
6. Place tip of tongue behind top front teeth.
7. Close eyes or leave them slightly open.

FOCUS
ON THE BREATH
AS IT FLOWS IN & OUT
OF THE BODY

BECOME AWARE
OF SENSATIONS INSIDE
& OUTSIDE THE BODY

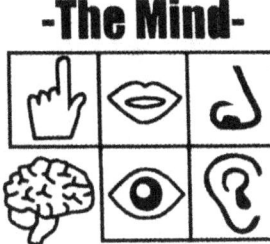

❋ Give instructions about MMP practice using the guide.

❋ Questions and answers.

IWS Mindfulness Process

❋ Start with MMP practice.

❋ Invite participants to close their eyes, if they have not already done so.

❋ Encourage participants to become aware of sensations inside and outside their body.

❋ Encourage participants to focus on the breath and bring into the MIND space sensations, one-by-one all six senses.

❋ Become aware the sensation happening inside and outside the body. Invite them to focus their awareness on one sensation, be with, accept, and move on to another sensation. Return to the former sensation and see if they notice any change. When they notice any change in sensation, it's *letting go*. Even if it's a very subtle difference, it becomes the process of *letting go* of the holding on they experience in the moment.

❋ Change in any sensory: Seeing, tasting, touching, smelling, hearing, thinking mind, is *letting go*.

❋ Be with each sensation fully and completely. Invite them to open their mind to the experience without judging right or wrong, good or bad, pleasure or pain.

❋ Invite participants to open their eyes if they are ready and come back to the space by subtle body engaging movement.

❋ Go around the room, encouraging each person to share their experience with the process.

❋ Questions and answers about MMP practice or process.

BETWEEN CLASS PRACTICE

✻ Encourage participants to maintain a daily sitting practice using MMP's *Mindful Meditation Guide* provided.

✻ Encourage participants to fully explore all six senses, be with sensation, accept sensation, and move on to another sensation. Then, coming back to a sensation and analyzing any change that might have happened. This is *letting go*.

✻ Encourage participants to experience sensations as a new sense without origin, not belonging to them—simply a sense with a MIND free from right or wrong, good or bad, pleasure or pain.

✻ Pair the sitting practice with the sensation process as much as they can and become aware if their perceptions about their world, or the world around them, shift—even for a moment, to a more expansive, questioning, observing state.

TAKE AWAY

Letting go is a process of be with, accept, and move on. Understanding that sensations have the capacity to influence the *who we have become*, and the transformation occurs in redefining by connecting with our true nature. Our true nature is open, expansive, non-judging, peaceful, and a calm state.

Experiencing *letting go* of some small part of holding on brings light to the ability to manifest change in our life. Holding on manifests rigid unchanging beliefs about ourselves and others that only promote stuck, closed, and ever-deepening patterns of suffering.

MINDFULNESS MEDITATION PROGRAM

Notes

"The unchanging connection we human beings share with every part of our planet is Consciousness."

Clifford L. Carter

Neutralizing Dis-Ease

MINDFULNESS-BASED AUTHORIZED CURRICULUM ~ FIRST EDITION

Class Eleven: Wrap up

Theme– Wrap up

NEUTRALIZING DIS-EASE IS A PROCESS facilitated by connecting with our true nature through *Mindfulness Meditation Program* practice. The first step is connection with our body through sensation. Next, we explore sensations with an open, non-judging mind. As we navigate sensations without judging, we see the subtle ways in which change occurs. The change proves impermanence, as well as brings light to the *holding on* that can manifest unnecessary suffering.

When we feel a sensation, fully explore the sensation as if we are on an inner safari without knowing the outcome. We begin to understand the way our mind processes information and acts upon that information.

The feeling of the information in the MIND, generates the process of *holding* as *this is who I am*, or *pushing away* as *this is not who I am*. Only the space between *holding* and *pushing away* lives the calm waters of the MIND. Free from grasping and aversion, the true state of the MIND is calm, at ease, processing information without clinging.

As I use MMP practice, when sensations trigger an experience from my past I am able to calmly explore the happenings, be with the experience, accept the experience as the past, and move on to the next sensation that arises.

The process of becoming aware, be with, accept, and move on to another sensation happens in the MIND. What follows is the real magic.

When acceptance happens in the MIND, the body follows by letting go. The process: Sensation, Thought, Action, Acceptance, Letting Go.

TIME RECOMMENDATIONS

※ Overview: approximately 20-30 minutes.

※ Sensing, sensing deeply process: 45 minutes.

※ Discussion 15-30 minutes.

※ Homework assignment and questions: 15-20 min.

※ Total time for class: 1 hour.

Mindfulness Meditation Program

MINDFUL MEDITATION GUIDE

1. Choose a comfortable seated position.
2. Maintain spinal integrity.
3. Slightly tuck chin.
4. Rest hands on thighs.
5. Relax jaw.
6. Place tip of tongue behind top front teeth.
7. Close eyes or leave them slightly open.

FOCUS
ON THE BREATH
AS IT FLOWS IN & OUT
OF THE BODY

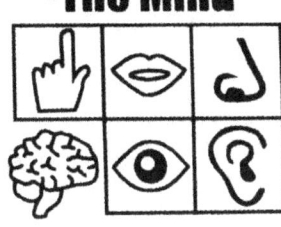

BECOME AWARE
OF SENSATIONS INSIDE
& OUTSIDE THE BODY

❋ Give instructions about MMP practice using the guide.

❋ Questions and answers.

Mindfulness Process

❋ Start with MMP practice.

❋ Invite participants to close their eyes, if they have not already done so.

❋ Encourage participants to become aware of sensations inside and outside their body.

❋ Encourage participants to focus on the breath and bring into the MIND space sensations, one-by-one all six senses.

❋ Become aware of sensation happening inside and outside the body. Focus awareness on one sensation, be with, accept, and move on to another sensation. Return to the former sensation and see if they notice any change. When they notice any change in sensation, it is *letting go*. Even if it's a very subtle difference, it becomes the process of *letting go* of the *holding on* they experience in the moment.

❋ Change in any sensory: seeing, tasting, touching, smelling, hearing, thinking mind is *letting go*.

❋ Be with each sensation fully and completely. Open the MIND to the experience without judging right or wrong, good or bad, pleasure or pain.

❋ Invite participants to open eyes if they are ready and come back to the space by subtle body engaging movement.

❋ Go around the room, encouraging each person to share their experience with the process.

❋ Questions and answers about MMP practice or process.

BETWEEN CLASS PRACTICE

❋ Encourage participants to maintain a daily sitting practice using MMP's *Mindful Meditation Guide* provided.

❋ Encourage participants to fully explore all six sensations, be with sensation, accept sensation, and move on to another sensation. Then, come back to a sensation and analyze any change that might have happened. The change is *letting go*.

❋ Encourage participants to experience each sensation as if it were a new sense without origin, not belonging to them, simply a sense with a MIND free from right or wrong, good or bad, pleasure or pain.

❋ Pair the sitting practice with the sensation process as much as they can and invite them to become aware if their perceptions about their world, or the world around them, shift—even for a moment, to a more expansive, questioning, observing state.

TAKE AWAY

After completing the process of *Neutralizing Dis-Ease,* my hope is a greater understanding of who you are in every moment of every day in your life from this moment on. We are a product of our environment, people, places, and things that form us to the *who we have become*—layers upon layers, day after day, year after year. Environmental pollution infects our one true nature inherent within us all.

This nature born with is unchanging calm, waiting for the time we clear away the debris that has been covering self. The process, though not easy, is a simple practice of meditation, which slows the mind and calms the nervous system, followed by mindful awareness being the tool of change.

We begin to notice an *okay* state, where a past-triggering thought-formed grasping/aversion are replaced by a feeling of belonging and accepting. The feeling of belonging to our true nature manifested by *letting go* of the tethers that informed past experience, allows us to be truly free.

MINDFULNESS MEDITATION PROGRAM

Notes

_____

_____

_____

_____

_____

_____

_____

_____

_____

_____

> *"Who we are starts on the inside and slowly works its way to the surface"*

Meaning, as layers upon layers of self-sensing consciousness unfold, our true nature has the opportunity and ability to work its way to the surface. As we connect with true nature through mindfulness meditation, more and more we take our nature from the cushion in to our daily life, transforming the WHO WE HAD BECOME based on environmental pollutants to true self or true nature. Peace, calm, open, expansive replace stuck, rigid beliefs that hold us to an old, mindless state.

Thank you for attending this class and course, and may the world become a better place, one soul at a time.

Neutralizing Dis-Ease

Mindfulness-Based Authorized Curriculum ~ First Edition

Evaluation Form

Date of Presentation: _____

Presenter's Name: _____

Please complete the evaluation your feedback is valuable to us and is appreciated.

IWS is committed to continual improvement and suggestions will be considered for future training needs.

What did you enjoy most about the class?

_____

_____

_____

_____

What did you learn that you anticipate using in your everyday life?

How will you implement this practice into your life?

Neutralizing Dis-Ease

MINDFULNESS-BASED AUTHORIZED CURRICULUM ~ FIRST EDITION

CRITERIA STRENGTH	STRONGLY DISAGREE 1	DISAGREE 2	AGREE 3	STRONGLY AGREE 4
Training was relevant to my needs.				
Materials provided were helpful.				
Training length was sufficient.				
Content was well organized.				
Questions were encouraged.				
Instructions were clear and understandable.				
Training met my expectations.				

Neutralizing Dis-Ease

MINDFULNESS-BASED AUTHORIZED CURRICULUM ~ FIRST EDITION

About Clifford Carter

MEDITATION HAS BEEN A BIG part of my life for a very long time, learning and understanding self through the practice. Monasteries and Buddhist centers enabled me to see the world through a different lens. Immersing myself in meditation was the way back to my true nature. The obstacle to self, or true nature, was patterning. The idea that there are preset rules handed down from generation to generation fueled my need to let go of the *who I had become*. The *who I had become* was based on environmental pollutants—environmental pollutants defined as people, places, and things. This curriculum is my way of sharing the process back to self—accepting and letting go of patterning that tethers us to the *who we have become*.

Clifford L. Carter is the founder of the non-profit organization, INNER WARRIOR SPIRIT, and currently facilitates and teaches meditation practices at his Colorado property.

www.ingramcontent.com/pod-product-compliance
Lightning Source LLC
Chambersburg PA
CBHW062034120526
44592CB00036B/2095